50 THING
BOOK
REVIEWS FROM READERS

I recently downloaded a couple of books from this series to read over the weekend thinking I would read just one or two. However, I so loved the books that I read all the six books I had downloaded in one go and ended up downloading a few more today. Written by different authors, the books offer practical advice on how you can perform or achieve certain goals in life, which in this case is how to have a better life.

The information is simple to digest and learn from, and is incredibly useful. There are also resources listed at the end of the book that you can use to get more information.

50 Things To Know To Have A Better Life: Self-Improvement Made Easy!

Author Dannii Cohen

This book is very helpful and provides simple tips on how to improve your everyday life. I found it to be useful in improving my overall attitude.

50 Things to Know For Your Mindfulness & Meditation Journey
Author Nina Edmondso

Quick read with 50 short and easy tips for what to think about before starting to homeschool.

50 Things to Know About Getting Started with Homeschool by Author Amanda Walton

I really enjoyed the voice of the narrator, she speaks in a soothing tone. The book is a really great reminder of things we might have known we could do during stressful times, but forgot over the years.

Author Harmony Hawaii

There is so much waste in our society today. Everyone should be forced to read this book. I know I am passing it on to my family.

50 Things to Know to Downsize Your Life: How To Downsize, Organize, And Get Back to Basics

Author Lisa Rusczyk Ed. D.

Great book to get you motivated and understand why you may be losing motivation. Great for that person who wants to start getting healthy, or just for you when you need motivation while having an established workout routine.

50 Things To Know To Stick With A Workout: Motivational Tips To Start The New You Today

Author Sarah Hughes

50 THINGS TO KNOW ABOUT BEING A HIGH SCHOOL ENGLISH TEACHER

A Guide from a Teacher

Kelly Hawkins

CZYK Publishing Since 2011.

50 Things to Know

Lock Haven, PA
ISBN: 9798597878270

50 THINGS TO KNOW ABOUT BEING A HIGH SCHOOL ENGLISH TEACHER

BOOK DESCRIPTION

Are you thinking of becoming a high school English teacher? Are you curious about what skills you need to be an effective educator? Are you wondering about how to build and maintain important relationships with students and colleagues? If you answered yes to any of these questions then this book is for you...

50 Things to Know about Being a High School English Teacher, by Kelly Hawkins, offers an honest description of teaching English at the high school level. Most books on teaching only tell you about the positive aspects of the profession. Although there's nothing wrong with that, education is a complex world to navigate, and people should enter a teaching career armed with as much accurate information as possible.

In these pages you'll discover one educator's experience over the last twenty-two years. This book will help you learn what it takes to successfully work with adolescents on a daily basis.

By the time you finish this book, you will know how to prepare for the academic year, how to manage the various roles teachers play, how to cope with the challenges of teaching, and how to connect with your students and colleagues. So grab YOUR copy today. You'll be glad you did.

TABLE OF CONTENTS

DEDICATION

To Mom and Dad – my first and best teachers

To all of my educators, from kindergarten through graduate school, that inspired me.

To Kathy Mouneimneh – the best mentor anyone could ever hope to have.

And to my fellow teachers that rose to the immense challenges of 2020 – you are warriors.

ABOUT THE AUTHOR

Kelly Hawkins has worked in education for the last twenty-two years. While earning her Bachelor of Arts degree from Bay Path University, she was asked by one of her professors to become an academic and writing tutor. This experience made her want to pursue a career as a high school English teacher. She earned her Master of Arts in Teaching and certification from Elms College while simultaneously working as a teacher assistant for a fifth grade class. Although she enjoyed interacting with the younger students, and it provided a great deal of experience, educating teenagers was what she ultimately wanted to do.

She completed her practicum at Agawam High School in Massachusetts and then received a position at Enrico Fermi High School in Connecticut. She missed AHS, however, so she returned there as a full time member of the English department the following year. She has taught in Agawam for the last eighteen years. She has worked with students of all abilities in grades nine through twelve during her tenure there, teaching a variety of core and elective courses.

In addition to being a full time high school English teacher, Kelly has worked as an adjunct professor, a writing tutor, and a teacher consultant for the Western Mass Writing Project. She has conducted workshops for fellow educators about writing across the curriculum and sharing best practices. She established a Writing Center at Agawam High School in 2019. Recently, she has completed several freelance writing projects and is hoping to pursue voice over work in the near future.

Being an English teacher, she clearly loves reading and writing but also enjoys watching films and crime shows. Her favorite thing to do, however, is spend time with her husband and their puppy. They reside in Western Massachusetts.

You can find her on Facebook.

INTRODUCTION

"What is a teacher? I'll tell you: it isn't someone who teaches something, but someone who inspires the student to give of her best in order to discover what she already knows."

Paulo Coelho

Teaching, like life, is a series of extremes. There will be days when you are certain that you have answered your calling and have found your dream job. There will also be days when you want to quit and run screaming from the school building. You will have moments of immense confidence in your abilities, followed by serious doubt. Failures will be balanced with victories, and the memories of smiles will help you get through the tears. The student that tested your patience yesterday will make you laugh today. Even though there is a routine, every day is different. Teaching is so much more than a career choice – it truly becomes a lifestyle – and navigating your way through the ups and downs can be a struggle.

It takes a special kind of person with a number of specific characteristics to be an effective educator. Teaching is the profession that helps to create all others. When done correctly, it is one of the most rewarding vocations. However, people need to hear the truth of it too – the challenges, the heartache, the failures, and the frustration. Teaching is exhausting. There will be times when you have nothing left to give, but you will be asked to do more, and you will somehow rise to the occasion. Your students depend on you for so much more than academics.

With the increasing number of responsibilities and expectations, teaching has lost its magic for some. Teacher burn out is a serious concern. Retaining certified, enthusiastic, and dedicated teachers is becoming more difficult. This guide is meant to give the reader an honest look at education. There are amazing aspects of it, yet there are tremendous difficulties. It can be a fulfilling lifelong career for some. Others may need to walk away when the joy is gone, and that is completely understandable.

Hopefully by reading these pages, you gain some insight into being a teacher – perhaps it will be discovering a new classroom activity, a surprising aspect of the job, or a different way to help your students. The best lesson that you could receive from it, however, would be to learn something about yourself.

PRIOR TO READING

We all have our own unique teaching journey. The following techniques have been successful for me and my students. Many things depend on the type of district in which you work, the culture of your school, and the kinds of students, co-workers, and administrators you have. Take whatever you can from the subsequent pages and adapt it to fit your own teaching situation.

I use a traditional teaching approach that I wholeheartedly believe still works. Therefore, the following advice does not focus on technology in the classroom or the latest educational methods, but rather on the importance of preparation, needed skills, and ways to build relationships. These recommendations have served me well over the last twenty-two years. They are valuable and worthy of being shared.

PART A: PREPARATION FOR THE SCHOOL YEAR

1. SUPPLIES

Before the school year starts, obtain the necessary materials. New folders, notebooks, binders, pens, pencils, and notepads mentally signify a brand new year and a fresh start. Most, if not all, teachers buy at least some of these materials with their own money. If your district can provide the needed supplies, you are extremely fortunate.

Find out what resources will be offered and what will need to be purchased. In addition to countless supplies such as scissors, paper clips, tape, staplers, dry erase markers, and paper, two things that you should always have are boxes of tissues and bandages. You will have students ask for these items more than you ever imagined.

Some stores offer a teacher discount or have a reward program for educators. Whether you are shopping online or in person, check to see what deals are available. If you belong to a teachers' union (which I strongly recommend) they often partner with

businesses to give teachers price reductions as well.
Don't be afraid to ask!

2. SETTING UP YOUR CLASSROOM

Once you have your supplies, it is time to set up
your classroom - if you are lucky enough to have one.
When I began teaching, there were more English
teachers than classrooms, so I was what they call a
"floating teacher." I was given a cart on which I kept
all of my supplies and traveled from room to room. I
tried to make the best of it, but after three years, I was
longing for a more permanent space.

Finally, after some retirements, I was able to
obtain a classroom of my own. Now that I have
control over my room, I work hard to give it a
welcoming atmosphere. I open the window shades as
much as I can to let in the most natural light. The
space is clean and well organized. The bulletin
boards are covered with bright paper and borders.
Film posters, inspirational quotes, and recycled
calendar pictures are displayed. There is a list of the
most important classroom and school rules posted as
a visual reminder for students.

Discover what works for you as far as decorating. Be careful to follow any fire code your building has, however, before you begin. Some schools limit the amount of flammable materials that can be placed on the walls.

As you continue to organize your room, think about item location. For example, having a pencil sharpener and the waste basket at the back of the room will limit disruptions. Be certain that paper, tissues, and other supplies are easily accessible for the students.

Create a pleasant environment with extra lighting and shelves full of books that the students may borrow if they finish an assignment early. Design a place where students feel comfortable and look forward to coming every day.

3. TEACHER WARDROBE

The appearance of your classroom is not the only thing that your students will notice, especially teenagers. Just as they have most likely gone "back to school shopping" for new clothes, teachers can update their wardrobe too. Buying outfits that make you feel confident can mentally prepare you for the year.

Even if your school does not have a strict dress code for staff, you will want to dress appropriately, especially if you are a young teacher. Dressing to look older and more professional will help to distinguish you from your pupils.

You can dress professionally but still be comfortable, which is my preference, especially in my chosen footwear. I work in the largest one-story school building in Massachusetts. I do quite a bit of walking during the day. I like flat, comfortable shoes and loose fitting clothing. Dressing in layers is a good idea too, as the temperature in your classroom and other sections of the building will probably not be consistent.

4. SAFETY DRILLS

Clothing choices can also be important for school safety drills. If there is a fire drill, will you have to walk across a wet grassy football field? Then perhaps having an extra pair of shoes in your closet is a good idea. Are the winters cold and snowy? If so, keep your coat (or at least a sweater) accessible so you can grab it before heading out the door. Having an extra umbrella on hand is wise as well.

Our school also has lockdown and barricade drills. During those moments, we have to move furniture around and then sit on the floor. Sometimes we need to evacuate the building and walk a short distance. Again, being comfortably dressed has aided me in these situations.

Whatever type of drills you have, pay attention and learn from them each time. Then you will be able to plan ahead and improve for the next one.

5. POLICIES AND PROTOCOLS

Knowing the proper procedures for drills and potential emergencies is extremely important. If you are a new teacher, acquaint yourself with the safety guidelines and ask questions. Even if you are an experienced teacher, review the rules to ensure that you have the most current information.

Familiarize yourself with the school rules and personnel policies also. Thoroughly read any student and staff handbooks that are provided to you. Ask for clarification when needed. Keep this information in a convenient place so you can refer to it quickly.

6. ORGANIZATION

In addition to safety information and school policies, there are so many more materials that you will need to keep track of; it can be overwhelming. Creating a personalized system of organization is essential. You may want to label different folders for important paperwork such as faculty meeting agendas, parent contacts, extra class lists, or discipline referrals. Store them in a safe place since they may contain confidential information. I also keep a detailed planner, and I constantly write myself notes as reminders throughout the day.

As a visual learner, I love to color code things. I have a specific folder for each class where I keep the assignments that need to be graded. I attempt to return papers to the students as soon as they are corrected, reducing the amount of paperwork on my desk.

Although we have an electronic grading system, I still keep an old-fashioned grade book. It gives me a back-up, should any issues arise with the technology. The portability makes it easier when checking off homework or a quick classwork assignment. Then when I have a moment, I put the grades into the computer. I also color code my gradebook to make it easier for me to read. Find what works the best for you with organization, and then make it a routine.

PART B: THE START OF THE SCHOOL YEAR

7. FIRST IMPRESSIONS

Once the preparation is complete, you will welcome your students. As in most situations, making a great first impression is very important. Be friendly and approachable. Stand outside your classroom to greet your kids with a smile as they enter your room. Then keep up that routine throughout the year. Sometimes you are the only trusted adult they have in their lives. They will look forward to receiving a genuinely warm greeting each day.

Typically, I teach mostly freshmen. My class is often one of the very first high school experiences they have, so I want to make it a great one. I use humor to put them at ease. I like to quickly learn their names and how to correctly pronounce them. When I take attendance for the first time, I repeat their names and ask if they prefer a nickname. Just these simple acts show your students how important they are from day one.

I also try my hardest not to mistakenly call a student by their older brother or sister's name or to judge them based on their sibling's behavior or academic performance. Each student is unique and should be considered as such.

8. INITIAL ACTIVITY

At the beginning of the year, I ask my students to answer introductory questions about themselves. This information allows me to get to know them fairly quickly – their likes and dislikes, interests, hobbies, talents, and learning styles. You need to show them that you have an interest in them as people, not just students.

Before they complete the questionnaire, however, I give them a "pop quiz," assuring them it does not count for a grade. I have them number their papers #1-20 and ask them twenty questions about me. Obviously, having just met me, they have no idea of the correct answers, but that is what makes it fun. They must guess and use their creativity. This activity breaks the ice and lets me see what kind of class I have as we go over the answers. I learn which kids want to participate, have a great sense of humor, are creative or competitive. They realize that I have my own personality traits, just like them. This traditional activity puts the kids at ease and lets me connect with them quickly.

After I share information with them, they are less reluctant to reciprocate. I carefully read the answers to their questionnaires and return them at the end of the year. Students enjoy seeing them after that much time has passed, because some of their answers have changed. They grow and mature quite a bit over the course of the year.

9. CLEAR EXPECTATIONS

After completing a fun ice-breaker activity, get down to business. Thoroughly go over your classroom policies, and ask if there are any questions. Have the students and their parents/guardians sign the last page, acknowledging that they have read and understood everything contained in the policies. Leave space for any written comments or concerns on the bottom of the last page as well.

Beginning the year with very clear expectations that are shared with students and parents is vital. If you intend for students to follow your rules, you must be clear of what those rules are and specify the consequences for breaking them. Be specific with your expectations and repeat them often. Post a list of the most important rules in the classroom where it is easily visible. Praise kids when they meet or exceed these expectations, and be sure to provide the given consequence when they do not. You must be as consistent as possible with your rules in order for them to work. Students should be expected to abide by these rules, even when you are not present.

10. SICK DAYS

Your students should be very clear on what your expectations are for their behavior when there is a substitute teacher. Being absent and leaving plans for someone else is much more difficult than going in to school. If you have minor discomfort and are not contagious, I would recommend "toughing it out." Then, at least you can accomplish what you had planned for the day.

If you must be out, for whatever reason, make sure you leave the substitute teacher detailed plans, the needed materials, and a contact person that can help. To ensure that your students complete their work, make the assignment count for a grade, even if you just check it quickly for classwork or participation points.

Having several sets of emergency plans prepared ahead of time is a good idea as well. They do not need to correspond to a particular curriculum unit. For example, students can write a creative piece using previously learned vocabulary or read a short story and write a summary of the plot.

Regardless of the plans you leave or the reason you are absent, your students should be well aware of your expectations for when there is a substitute.

Praise them if a positive report is left, and follow through with any consequence if rules are broken.

11. BACK TO SCHOOL NIGHT

In addition to students being aware of your classroom policies, their parents should be also. Soon after our students return to school, we hold our annual "Back to School Night" for the parents and guardians. Again, making a positive first impression is important. Stand outside the classroom door, welcome each parent with a smile, and set a friendly tone. Prepare what you will say ahead of time and have materials ready.

During this event, teachers present a brief overview of the textbooks and curriculum. I provide an extra copy of my classroom policies and make certain that parents have my contact information. In addition, I stress that the education of their children is a team effort. I encourage them to communicate with me about any questions or concerns.

Establishing a positive parent-teacher relationship from the beginning can make things run more smoothly during the year. Letting the parents know that you care about their children is one of the most important messages to get across during this initial meeting. Doing so makes them feel reassured that their children are in good hands.

12. BEFORE CURRICULUM

Now that your students and their parents know that you care about them, and you have clearly communicated your expectations, you can finally begin with the actual curriculum. I do not think you can successfully teach kids anything until you have a rapport with them. If you model the desired behavior, most of the time, the kids will follow your lead. They need to trust you and respect you. Be sincere with your students. They can spot an imposter a mile away. Being genuine enables you to connect with them, allowing you to better deliver the curriculum.

13. BUT NOT EVERYONE LOVES ENGLISH

I became an English teacher because I love to read and write. I quickly learned when I first began my career, however, that not everyone feels the same way. I discovered that even though some of my students do share my enthusiasm for English, others despise reading and writing and are reluctant to do it, because they lack confidence in their abilities.

My biggest challenges have been to first understand those differences and not take them personally. Then I try my best to encourage and motivate my students. I attempt to make my class interesting, engaging, and memorable, so that they look forward to coming to it every day, even if English is not their favorite or best subject. Creating a safe and welcoming space for them to enjoy their time in my classroom and learn something is my goal. If they end up appreciating literature and writing along the way, that is even better.

PART C: CHARACTERISTICS OF AN EFFECTIVE TEACHER

14. POSITIVITY

You must attempt to reach all of your kids, whether they like your class or not. Having a positive attitude and being optimistic is contagious. (Just as complaining and being negative is contagious.) If you express enthusiasm for your subject, then chances are more of your students will too. If they feel that they are in a safe environment and can trust you and their classmates, they are more likely to contribute. Once they are comfortable with positively participating in class, you can praise them for their effort. This approach will help to build their self-confidence, thus making them more prone to like your class and succeed in the course.

15. HUMOR

Another way to create a positive classroom atmosphere is to use and encourage appropriate humor. Students appreciate a teacher that can take a joke. Most teachers, in turn, enjoy when a student has a great sense of humor. However, it can be a challenge to make sure it does not go too far. You have to set boundaries for when kids can have fun and when they need to be more serious. This balance comes with experience. All jokes must be light-hearted and never at anyone's expense. They must also be school appropriate. A sense of humor will definitely benefit you when interacting with adolescents on a daily basis.

Humor may help you deal with all kinds of difficult school situations. A witty comment may diffuse tension during a faculty or department meeting. A clever pun may liven up a quiet lunch or a dull Professional Development session. Sharing laughter bonds people and creates joy. We all need that as much as possible.

16. FLEXIBILITY

In addition to having a sense of humor, another helpful trait as an educator is flexibility. Often times, unavoidable disruptions will occur. However, at other times you will be the one that changes the plans. Perhaps during a lesson, an important topic arises unexpectedly, and you want the students to continue their discussion of it, instead of moving on to the next activity. These unplanned "pop up" times are referred to as "teachable moments" and they can be very valuable.

Maybe the lesson you had planned does not even happen one day, because a world event occurred the night before. The class seems to want or even need to talk about it. If you can facilitate a civilized discussion that helps or teaches the kids, it can be constructive. Sometimes, those are the best moments. They are pure and unscripted.

Again, I cannot stress the importance of planning enough, especially when you are first starting out in your career, but do recognize that those plans will get interrupted. You may have designed a lesson for exactly the length of your class, but then a weather delay causes shortened class periods. Do you adapt and edit the lesson? Should you postpone your original agenda until the next day and scramble to come up with an alternative for today? Is it possible to add to the lesson and break it into two days? You must make the decision and work with it.

A plethora of things happen on a daily basis to cause us to have to switch gears. Always have a "Plan B," and perhaps even "Plans C- G." Having alternative ideas and being able to execute them is an imperative skill for teachers. Accept that there will be last minute changes and handle them. Sometimes that can get extremely frustrating, but it is a permanent part of the job. The more flexible you are with modifications, the easier your school life will be.

17. PATIENCE AND UNDERSTANDING

Being flexible is important, but in order to survive in teaching, you also need an exorbitant amount of patience and understanding. We are only human, and we have our bad days too, but try your best to be in a good mood each day and put any personal troubles to the side.

When your students are having difficulty, you should be understanding and attempt to help them however you can. For example, if a student is having a terrible day, perhaps not calling on him/her is the best option for that class. Maybe giving a student more one on one attention is what is needed. Knowing your kids and their moods allows you to make the best decisions for interacting with them.

It is not always easy to have patience, but it is crucial. Sometimes the kids who need the most love are those that exhibit the worst behavior. They go about getting your attention in the wrong way. Take a deep breath and keep calm, because giving in to their words or actions just exacerbates the situation. This is easier said than done on some days, I know, but our students depend on us to be consistent, patient, and understanding, even when it is challenging. You will not always succeed, but try your best.

18. EMPATHY

Empathy is another trait that will help you in many situations, but particularly in teaching. Recalling what high school was like helps me to understand my students' perspective. As teenagers, they usually think in the moment and situations can be exaggerated. An argument with a friend, a failing grade, or being punished by their parents can seem like the world is ending. You must acknowledge their feelings and tell them that things will improve. We are not to judge what is important to them. We just have to listen and try to help them through it.

A small act you can do when students are struggling is to leave notes on their desks (when the other students will not notice) with positive messages such as, "I hope your day gets better" or "Let me know if I can help in any way." I have seen the effect this simple gesture has on students. Sometimes it is a quick smile, or they come back after class to thank me, or even other times they will repay the favor when I have a bad day. Exhibiting empathy can be a lesson too.

19. HONESTY

Along with demonstrating empathy, be as honest as you can with your students. Obviously, you cannot share all information with them, but they are young adults. They deserve the truth whenever possible.

Being straightforward with your students creates an atmosphere of trust. If you are not feeling well, tell them, so they do not mistake your quiet demeanor as something they did wrong. If you do not know the answer to a question they ask, admit it. When you acknowledge that you do not have all of the answers, they will respect you more. No one is perfect. (Just be sure to find the missing answer and follow up with the kids later.) You may be the only person they trust, so you need to do everything in your power to be honest with them.

20. SHARE IMPORTANT INFORMATION

In your attempt to be honest with your students, inform them about school related issues. As mentioned earlier, I make certain that the students are well aware of the classroom and school rules, but you need to continue to be a reliable source of information.

In addition to the rules, make certain your students know when there will be a schedule change or an assembly. Inform them of fund raisers and picture day. Write weekly reminders up on the board and hang up fliers in a place reserved just for student information. When students know what to expect, it alleviates some of their anxiety. I often have kids thank me for sharing information with them, and that confirms its importance.

21. KIDS VERSES YOUNG ADULTS

Over time you will learn just how much information to share with your classes, depending upon what year they are. The span of time between ninth and twelfth grade brings differences in physical and mental development, maturity, responsibility, and experiences. Ninth graders should be given more specific information and guidance. However, you can speak more candidly with the upperclassmen.

Regardless of their year, they are still a mixture of children and young adults. They love to dress up for Halloween and look forward to pep rally. They enjoy receiving stickers on quizzes and tests when they have done well. Simultaneously, they desperately want to be treated as adults.

Students reach several milestones and rites of passage such as getting their driving licenses or their first jobs throughout high school, but they are not quite ready for full adulthood. You must keep this unique combination in mind when working with adolescents.

22. STUDENT INPUT

Even though these young adults sit in front of us each day, some teachers do not realize what a valuable resource they can be. After teaching for several years, your ideas can get stale.   When that happens, you can ask the students for their input, indicating that you value their thoughts and suggestions. Some of the best ideas that I still use came from former students. If you allow them to be part of the decision making process, it empowers them and builds their confidence. Let them make some decisions and have choices occasionally to take some control over their learning.

PART D: ROLES OF A TEACHER

23. THE HATS YOU WILL WEAR

As the world of education evolves, the demands on teachers steadily increase. For some of your students, you may fill the position of a parental figure. Not every child comes from a happy, intact family. You may be the only trusted adult they have in their lives. You need to take that, and the myriad of other roles you play, very seriously. You will not be "just" their teacher.

Teaching the curriculum seems to be a much smaller part of our job than it used to be. We now serve as coaches, nurses, psychologists, and police officers to a small degree. This is not to diminish the hard work that people of these professions actually do. I simply mean that you need to encourage your students, show them how to work together, and take care of them when they get sick or injured while on your watch. You need to address their mental health and their social and emotional well-being. You need to protect them during drills and lockdowns.

Your students are in your care for several hours each day. You will worry about the troubled ones when you cannot sleep at night. You will celebrate their victories with them and lament their failures. You are responsible for the whole student, not just their academic achievement.

24. MANDATED REPORTER

One of the most important roles teachers play is that of mandated reporter. We must share any evidence or even suspicion immediately when our students are being abused, neglected, or having suicidal thoughts. Not only is this good practice, but it is our legal obligation to report when we think our kids may be in danger.

Always communicate any concerns you have to the appropriate people – administrators, guidance counselors, whoever the contact is in your school. Make certain that you reach the appropriate person(s) as soon as possible and that you get some sort of response. It is always better to err on the side of caution in any situation where you are concerned about a student, for any reason. If it turns out to be nothing, no harm done, and you still did your job. If you have a suspicion and keep quiet, it can have dire consequences. Do not wait and do not remain silent.

25. STUDENT CHECK-INS

In addition to being mandated reporters, we need to monitor our students' social and emotional well-being as well as their academic success. This responsibility can be daunting. One quick way to touch base with your kids is to have them complete a "check-in." You can do this activity as often as you wish. The students complete a low-stakes free-write of at least half a page. That way, as long as they write the appropriate length, they will receive credit. They do not need to focus on proper spelling and grammar for this exercise, which enables them to write their thoughts more freely.

Some guiding questions might be to ask for positive and negative events that have taken place in their lives recently or things they are looking forward to in the near future. Students do not have to answer the provided questions. They can just write about how they are feeling in general. Most students like this activity. It gives them a chance to express their feelings without judgement, it is an easy participation grade, and they know that you genuinely care about them.

As the teacher, reading through their responses allows you to see how each of your students is doing.

You can encourage them, share in their joy, or reassure them that difficult times will pass. This exercise also establishes you as a safe and trusted person they can turn to for help.

26. CORRECTING LOAD

As an English teacher, along with all of the above responsibilities, you will have a great deal of written work to correct. The truth is you will be working on nights, weekends, and vacations, at least for the first several years of your career. This will be necessary to keep up with the enormous workload. Over time, you will find that you do not need to grade every single thing that your students do. You will also discover tips and tricks that make correcting a bit more manageable.

Looking for certain "Focus Correction Areas" or "FCA's" in an essay is a good habit. For example, if the students turn in a short research assignment, the focus of their grades can be on the citations and the Works Cited page. That way, you will not be pouring over their work and correcting every minor mistake. Both you and your students will be aware of the areas that will be targeted.

Another technique is to have the students write each paragraph of an essay separately. That way, you only have to correct one paragraph from each student at a time. Then they can edit their work, and when they turn in the final copy, most of their improvements should already have been made, saving you time and effort while grading.

27. FAST-PACED DAY

As a teacher, you exude an amazing amount of energy on correcting but also on many other daily obligations. (Multi-tasking is a necessity.) You constantly interact with your classes, administrators, and colleagues. On an average day, you present lessons, answer countless questions, and handle classroom management issues. Your free period is usually taken up by making photo copies, unjamming the machine, planning for the upcoming week, and answering emails. You may have time for a quick restroom stop, but that is doubtful. You will most likely have to wait until your lunch break, which is not quite a half-hour where I work.

After lunch, even though you are getting tired, you may have your most challenging classes. Just after settling your students down to work on their assignment, another student may arrive at your door in tears. You keep one eye on your class, while you try to console the upset student and call the guidance office to see if a counselor is available to come to your room.

After school, you probably have a department or faculty meeting. Perhaps students are staying for extra help. Maybe you are running the Book Club, because you are the advisor or you have seven letters of recommendation to write for seniors who are applying to colleges.

Sometimes you can have many ups and downs throughout the same day. There is always a great deal happening and a ton of responsibilities that need your attention. You will be exhausted at the end of a full day of teaching. If you are not, then you did something wrong.

PART E: SOME PROS AND CONS

28. ROUTINE VERSES VARIETY

There is a nice balance of having a set schedule and somewhat of a routine each day, but it never gets boring, as described above. Even though you have the same lesson planned, it may work very differently in the various classes that you have. Despite the fact that you were intending on making copies during your free period, you may be asked to cover a colleague's class instead. You can have a rough idea of what a day will bring, but you can never know for certain until it unfolds.

That variety is one of the greatest parts of this job. Each day is different. Actually each day, week, month, and marking period is a fresh beginning for you and your students. Inspire them (and yourself) to take advantage of those opportunities. We all make mistakes. We all have difficulties throughout the year, but if we help each other to look ahead and try our best, we can overcome some of those challenges.

29. JUDGEMENT AND CRITICISM

One unfortunate aspect of teaching is the constant condemnation. Many others (usually those outside of education) unfairly judge and openly criticize teachers. I try my best to not make any assumptions about other professions for one very important reason – I have never worked at any of them. I have no idea what an average day looks like for a bank teller, a butcher, a waitress, or a doctor, because I have never been any of those things. Yet many people feel they have the right to judge and harshly criticize what we do and how we do it. That has never made sense to me. Teachers help others to reach their goals. We have former students who become dental hygienists, engineers, musicians, artists, authors, and teachers themselves. Why is the profession that helps to create all others constantly targeted in a negative way?

I bring this point up to ensure a realistic description of teaching. It is one of the most negative features of the job, and it has always been there, at least in my experience. So many of us treat teaching as a lifestyle that defines us, rather than simply a chosen career. We give it our all each day to help our students. Yet, we have critics that tell us what we are doing does not matter, that we are doing it incorrectly, or that we do not work hard enough or long enough hours. I invite these critics to sign up to become a substitute teacher. Then they can experience first-hand how difficult it is. No one outside of education has the right to constantly judge us, just as we should not make any assumptions about other professions.

30. NEEDED BREAKS

One reason that others judge teaching may be for the perceived amount of "vacation" time that we have. However, they do not consider all of the hours we spend working at home once we leave the school building. Nor do they realize how many roles we actually fill on any given day.

Most of us have a great deal of curriculum that we are required to cover throughout the year. This task creates a significant amount of work, on top of fulfilling the previously mentioned responsibilities. Teachers need a tremendous work ethic and they should try to instill that in their students as much as possible; however, we are only human and need a break every once in a while.

You will be exhausted by Friday night each week. Perhaps not giving homework over the weekend occasionally will give your students (and you) a chance to catch up on some other chores. Ending class a few minutes early so that students may begin their homework, if they behave while doing so, gives you an opportunity to answer a few emails.

We work extremely hard and fit an incredible amount into a school day in addition to working during nights, weekends, and vacations. It is easy to become burned out in teaching. In an attempt to not let that happen, you must make time for yourself. Once you have been teaching long enough to have a handle on the lesson plans and correcting, try to give yourself at least one weeknight and one entire weekend day off from school work. Create a schedule over a vacation where you only have certain days or hours for planning and grading. Once your work is completed, you can fully enjoy the rest of your time.

I typically take the first two weeks of summer vacation to decompress from the year. I do not think about or look at anything school related. After that, then I can combine relaxing with completing a course or updating curriculum throughout the remainder of the summer. You must find ways to renew, refresh, and rejuvenate or you will not last long in education.

31. CONTROL OVER CURRICULUM

If you are given the opportunity to take part in updating the curriculum for a course, I would highly encourage it. Hopefully, you work in a district where teachers are still given a fair amount of autonomy. Having control over not just what we teach, but how we teach it, is very important.

When I first started teaching, as long as I covered the required units, I could plan and deliver the material in whatever way I saw fit. It certainly took a great deal of time to prepare for each day, but I was excited to use my creativity and individual style. I could also tailor lessons to fit the needs of my classes, because I knew my kids, their strengths, and where they needed improvement.

Recently there has been a push to make teachers much more "aligned." The amount of creativity that we are permitted to use has dwindled. My English teacher colleagues and I are required to make "departmentalized" exams. We are expected to use the same materials and present information in similar fashions for each unit we cover.

This change, in my opinion, is unfortunate. It does not serve the students well, and it has stripped us of feeling like we have any control over how we teach. When you present material in your own way, it is much more enjoyable. The students get more of a variety of teaching styles and strategies.

In education, it is well recognized that students have different ways of learning. Some are visual learners, some auditory, some kinesthetic and so on. We see the benefit to using differentiated instruction for our classes. It makes sense, and I support it. What I cannot understand, is why some people do not see that it is the same for teachers. We all had unique learning styles too, and now we teach differently. There is nothing wrong with that. We can utilize our individual strengths to best help our students. We just need to be given back our autonomy and trusted as professionals.

PART F: REFRESH YOUR LOVE OF TEACHING

32. TEACH DIFFERENT GRADE LEVELS

Once you have been teaching for a number of years, you may need to look for ways to revive your love of the job. Changing your schedule is one way to accomplish this goal. However, in the same way school districts vary in levels of teacher autonomy, they may also have different ways of scheduling teachers' courses. You may have to wait a few years to teach the classes you think you would like the most. I recommend that if and when you have the opportunity, you teach all grades and all abilities. You may be surprised at what age level with which you prefer to work. It will make you a better teacher to have such diverse experiences.

Each grade level has its pros and cons. Freshman students are often more timid, at least in the beginning, because the high school atmosphere is entirely new to them. You can help to guide them through the daily struggles as they acclimate to their surroundings. They need more attention and they have less maturity than the older students, but they are fun to work with and change a great deal from September to June.

Sophomores are like the "middle children" of the high school family. They are not the new freshman, and they are not yet upper classmen. They tend to get overlooked and lost in the shuffle sometimes. I have a soft spot for the tenth grade and try to make them feel recognized and noticed as much as I can.

Teaching the upperclassmen (juniors and seniors) can sometimes be more challenging because they are somewhat jaded. They know how the school works, and some of them are more than ready to leave and begin the next chapters of their lives. They are obviously much more mature than the freshman. You can speak to them on a different level. They are becoming young adults and realize more of what is happening. The conversations and class discussions have more depth to them with upperclassmen.

33. TEACH DIFFERENT ACADEMIC ABILITIES

Just like teaching different grade levels is beneficial, so is teaching students with varying abilities. Each academic level has pros and cons, but working with all of them will broaden your experience as an educator, and again, you may like working with one group more than you ever thought, so try them all.

Special Education students need some accommodations made to their assignments and grading. The required paperwork for these students can be more time-consuming, but I often find that these kids work tremendously hard. They know what things do not come easily to them, and they are tenacious about succeeding. Also, in some cases, you get the opportunity to work with a co-teacher who is certified in Special Education. Working with another teacher in the room as a team is extremely advantageous and can be a wonderful experience.

Teaching students in honors or advanced placement courses is also enjoyable. Typically, the classroom management is easier, and they are focused on the academics. They are sometimes more interested in the subject matter, and you are able to cover the curriculum at a faster pace. They can be a lot more competitive with each other and tend to expect higher grades, however.

Working with the college preparatory level can be the best of both worlds. You will typically have a mix of ability and behavior, and sometimes the chemistry of the class works out very well. Some students may positively influence the others. When this happens, consider yourself an extremely lucky teacher. When it does not, it can make for a long year.

34. TEACH NEW COURSES

Although it takes a tremendous amount of planning to teach a new course, it can be a wonderful challenge and help keep your teaching fresh. Do not let yourself become stagnant by teaching the same course for too long. If you still enjoy it, and are implementing new lessons and updated materials, then stay with it. If not, it may be time for a switch.

Sometimes, you may not have the choice, and a course will be assigned to you. Whatever the reason, when you teach a brand new class (or one that you have not taught in a long time) do not be afraid to ask for help. Seek out colleagues that currently teach that course. Collaborate with them. If possible, observe those teachers' classes to see how they present the material.

In addition, perhaps completing some Professional Development or using lesson planning websites will make you feel more comfortable. If you have any input into the curriculum, be sure to include a variety of literature from authors of different backgrounds. Diversity and representation is a must.

35. WORK WITH A STUDENT TEACHER OR BE A MENTOR

Another wonderful way to refresh your love of teaching is to mentor a new employee or to work with a student teacher. After all, someone had to do the same for you. When you are paired with someone that is just beginning their teaching career, it is beneficial for the both of you.

Brand new teachers/student teachers will have tons of questions and concerns. Make them feel more at ease by answering their questions and providing the support they need. Reassure them they are not alone and that you encountered similar struggles when you first began teaching.

They in turn, will remind you why you became a teacher. Their excitement and optimism will be contagious and will allow you to see things from a different perspective and break free from the rut. Seeing a new teacher interact with students can be rewarding and remind us why we are there – for the kids. Hopefully, it is a positive experience for both parties, and it may even produce a life-long friendship.

PART G: ADVICE FOR CONNECTING WITH STAFF AND STUDENTS

36. THE IMPORTANCE OF COMMUNICATION

When working with a student teacher or mentoring a new hire, constant communication is imperative. Strong correspondence skills are actually needed in every aspect of education. You must clearly convey your thoughts and ideas with your students and their parents, co-workers, and administrators. In turn, you need to listen to, acknowledge, and reply to their comments, questions, and concerns.

For example, if there is an issue with a student, parents should be contacted as soon as possible. Copies of discipline referrals and notes of any phone conversations or meetings should be dated and kept on file. Documentation is extremely important when working with so many stakeholders. A paper trail allows you to keep track of the things that you have done to help the student, keeps administrators informed, and shows parents how you have been trying to assist their child.

Communicating for positive reasons is beneficial too. Parents love to receive an email letting them know that their son or daughter did a wonderful job on a project or has significantly improved with his/her behavior in class. These messages illustrate that you want their child to succeed as much as they do, and you truly care about your students' progress and well-being.

Administrators also need strong communication skills. Updating their staff on school-related issues is extremely helpful and should be done often. Detailed information received in a timely manner makes our jobs a little easier. Being the first to receive important news makes us feel as though we are being treated professionally. A well informed staff works at their best level.

37. ASK FOR HELP

When important information is not automatically provided, you must ask for it. When you are struggling with a problem, tell someone. No matter how long you have been teaching, you do not have all the answers. There will be times when things change and teachers flounder, no matter how many years they have had in the classroom. We never stop learning. Just like we tell our students, we must remember to ask for help when we need it. Asking for assistance shows that you want to do something correctly and gain knowledge.

Did your school get a new grading software program? Ask a tech savvy colleague to show you how to use it if you are struggling. Are you having difficulty coming up with an engaging way to begin a unit with your classes? Ask someone in your department that teaches the same course for ideas. Do you need extra support when using databases for research purposes? Ask the librarian for pointers. Never be afraid to request assistance.

38. RECIPROCATE KINDNESS WITH CO-WORKERS

Knowing when to ask for guidance or advice is definitely a helpful skill; however, you need to make sure that you provide assistance to others just as often. Try to be the type of colleague that co-workers turn to when they need support. Find fellow teachers that you can always depend on and offer the same to them.

For example, when you have to be absent, ask a trusted colleague to print out your plans and help the substitute teacher. Then, when he/she has to be out, you can repay the favor. This friend can also be your ally when you need a bathroom break. Sometimes waiting for our free period, lunch, or the end of the day to use the restroom is just not possible. Having a teacher nearby that you can trust to supervise your class for a few minutes is extremely valuable. Again, reciprocate the kindness. Collegiality makes a challenging profession more manageable.

39. TREAT EVERYONE WITH RESPECT

In addition to working well with your fellow educators, you should build a rapport with your administrators, librarians, secretaries, custodians, and lunchroom staff. Many people make a school run, and they are all equally important. It does not matter what title they hold, they should be treated kindly and in a respectful manner. Again, positive working relationships make the difficult job of teaching more tolerable.

40. TEACHERS' LOUNGE

A place you may develop some of these positive working relationships may be the teachers' lounge. Depending upon the culture of your school, it can be a wonderful respite. Perhaps it offers the promise of fresh coffee and pleasant conversation. However, it may potentially be a room of toxicity and gossip. Be careful. Scope out the space and see how you feel when you are in there.

The hope is, that it is a spot where you can get some work done during your free period if you share your classroom with another teacher. Having a quiet space is important. If the lounge is too crowded, try the library. Find a place where you feel comfortable when you need to get work done if you cannot be in your own classroom. If the lounge is a location where you can complete your work or share some laughs and encouragement with your co-workers, go as much as you can.

It can often be a place where teachers gather to complain and vent frustrations. Although that is natural, if it happens too often, it is best to limit your visits there. Other times, it may be full of left over birthday cake and stale Halloween candy. If you are on a diet, you may want to avoid this spot altogether.

You will have to determine whether the positives outweigh the negatives and if the teachers' lounge is the right place for you.

41. FIND POSITIVE ASPECTS OF EVERYONE

If you do encounter some less than personable folks in the teachers' lounge, find some positive aspects of their personality. Focus on the good in others. Now, it may be more difficult or take longer with some people. However, looking for the good is always the better choice. This habit applies to administrators, colleagues, students, parents, and even yourself sometimes. Concentrate on the positive characteristics that people have. Mention these traits to show people that you have noticed them.

The more you focus on the good in people, the easier it will be to work with them. This is especially true of the kids that give you the most trouble. If you model this behavior of pointing out people's positive qualities, it becomes contagious. Students will pick up on it and start to emulate you, creating a much more pleasant atmosphere.

42. CLASS COMPLIMENTS

I have a favorite annual activity that encourages students to focus on the best aspects of themselves and their classmates. Just prior to the holiday break, I give the students a list of the names of everyone in the class. They are instructed to write two compliments below each name, even their own. Initially some of them are opposed to the idea, but they complete the assignment anyway. They must write the compliments down anonymously. When they are finished, they turn them in, and I make certain that they are complete and appropriate.

Between December and February whenever I have a few free minutes, I cut the paper with the compliments into strips. (If you are fortunate enough to have a student intern, this is a great task for them to help you complete.) Each student receives the compliments in a small gift bag on or near Valentine's Day.

Even the students who were hesitant to take part in the activity love the results. Once the students have received their bags and begin to read the compliments from their classmates, the smiles begin to spread. Then the laughter starts, and the excitement sets in. They have a wonderful time sharing the compliments with their friends or kids who sit near them. It is a special activity that shows the students others care about them. Former students often tell me that they still have their compliments after a number of years, and it was one of their favorite activities.

43. A DIFFERENT LIGHT

Sometimes you need to see students outside of your classroom to discover their best traits. One student may be extremely shy in class, but he/she performs a fantastic solo in the band concert. Another may not have the highest average, but he/she has the lead role in the school play and receives a standing ovation on opening night.

You should attend student events and support activities throughout the year. Having school spirit and pride for the institution in which you work is vital. It shows your kids that you care about what they do inside as well as outside of the classroom. Go to as many sporting events, concerts, art shows, and plays as you can, especially when students make a point of telling you about them. Going to these events allows you to see your students in a completely different way.

These kids have a lot of interests. You should make an effort to find out what they are and support them. By asking about their weekends, you can see who participates in school sponsored activities. Those that do not may have jobs or spend hours at the dance studio which takes up their time. Get to know your students. You will all benefit from the experience.

44. A REMINDER FOR ADMINISTRATORS

Just as teachers should get to know their students, administrators should get to know their teachers. The best administrators are those that keep in mind all of the challenges that teachers face and attempt to help them with those struggles. Teachers need to feel appreciated and supported. Their voices must be heard, their feelings must be validated, and their needs must be met. If administrators know their teachers well, this help may be easier to provide.

Principals were once teachers themselves, so they know what it was like; they just need to recall that as often as they can. Being a teacher and being an administrator are two separate jobs, but they have many of the same goals. If there is a strong partnership between teachers and administrators, the school will run more smoothly.

Administrators need support and appreciation too. Teachers have never been principals, so again, utilizing empathy is very important. Principals have difficult jobs and experience a great deal of stress just like teachers. They have tremendous responsibility. They need to know that they can trust their staff to be hard working professionals that put the students first. Having mutual respect and understanding between staff and administration is essential for a positive work environment.

PART H: AS THE YEAR WINDS DOWN

45. END OF THE YEAR CLEANING

As the academic year draws to a close, and you reflect on the above advice, one task that you want to be sure to complete is a thorough cleaning of your classroom. Accumulating a ton of materials does not take long, and sometimes we have difficulty throwing things away. Space is limited, so carefully choose what to keep and what to discard. Go through your classroom and purge what you no longer use. Clean out filing cabinets and computer files. Make room wherever you can, and recycle what no longer serves a purpose. Take photos of exemplary projects, instead of keeping the originals. Pack things away neatly and label boxes. Get in the habit of storing supplies in the same place at the end of each year. This process allows you to review all that you and your students have accomplished and will also help make the set-up of your room at the start of the year more manageable.

46. KEEP MOMENTOS

As you sort through the things you want to get rid of, be certain not to throw out the positive emails, notes, cards, letters, drawings, and gifts that you receive from your students and their parents. Keep them in a safe place and look at them often, especially on days when you are having doubts about whether or not teaching is the right profession for you. There may be several of those days. You will doubt yourself. Others will judge you. You will feel like you are not making a difference. Then you will look at some kind note from a student, and it reminds you why you keep trying day in and day out. These small tokens are priceless.

47. TEACHER EVALUATIONS

Other items to keep are student evaluations. At the end of the year (or the semester, if it is a half-year course), give your students the opportunity to anonymously evaluate your teaching. Ask them several specific questions with which you are the most concerned. You must have a thick skin and take what they write with a grain of salt. They are in essence, experts at some things, however, because they have sat in your classroom for many days and observe more than you may think. They are brutally honest. You may be pleasantly surprised by some of their answers. Others may be a bit upsetting or disappointing. Either way, you will definitely learn from their responses. Hopefully, you will make the needed adjustments to keep growing and improving as a teacher.

48. LEARN FROM YOUR STUDENTS

Teaching means that you will never stop learning. Gaining insight from student evaluations is just one lesson. There will be new technology and curriculum. School rules will shift and evolve. The students themselves will differ in some ways as the years progress. These changes only mean that we have more to learn ourselves. Yes, we teach our students lessons – academic as well as life – but they teach us a great deal in return.

Ask students about the latest slang or pop culture. They love "educating" adults. (Just make sure they are telling you accurate information.) If there is a new TikTok dance that they are all doing, ask them about it. If it is appropriate, they may even teach it to you. Find ways to bond with your students and learn from them. They can be very good teachers.

49. ATTEND GRADUATION

Another end of the year tradition you should adopt is attending graduation. So many teachers contribute to the education of one student. As a high school teacher, I fully realize that many educators came in line before me to help shape my students into who they have become. Graduating is a special rite of passage for these young adults with which you have spent so much time. What an honor it is to see them walk across the stage to receive the diploma that they worked so hard to earn. The event culminates their previous efforts and highlights all of the possibilities of their futures. As the final event of the year, it gives you a way to wish your students well before they enter the next phase of their lives.

50. KEEP IN TOUCH

With social media, it is now easier than ever to keep in touch with people. Make certain you follow the rules of your school, such as not communicating with students until after they graduate, but once they do, stay in touch. Allow them to send you a request to connect. (I never reach out to former students first.) You can continue to view their accomplishments. It has been such a pleasure to see former students earn their college degrees, join the military, begin their careers, buy homes, start families – or whatever other goals or milestones they have reached.

Staying in touch with kids also allows me to continue to help them. They can reach out if they need a letter of recommendation for a job. Some may even want to enter the field of education. They can request class observations or even to complete their practicum with me. Whatever the case may be, it has been wonderful maintaining relationships with former students as they become adults. Just like looking at those positive notes and letters, seeing kids succeed long after they were in your classroom is incredibly gratifying. After all, building and maintaining relationships is the foundation of teaching.

OTHER HELPFUL RESOURCES

Web English Teacher – a wide variety of lesson plans, activities, and materials for different areas of English including: literature, grammar, writing, poetry, drama, and Shakespeare

https://www.varsitytutors.com/englishteacher

National Council of Teachers of English – resources such as lesson plans, books, journals, and online learning opportunities

https://ncte.org/

newsela – a large variety of current event texts for several subjects with different reading levels and activities

newsela.com

COMMONLIT – an extensive collection of free reading passages; ways to track student progress

commonlit.org

POETRY OUT LOUD – instructions on how to organize and judge classroom and school competitions; a collection of poems and lesson plans about poetry. poetryoutloud.org

READ OTHER

50 THINGS TO KNOW

BOOKS

50 Things to Know

Stay up to date with new releases on Amazon:

https://amzn.to/2VPNGr7

50 Things to Know

We'd love to hear what you think about our content! Please leave your honest review of this book on Amazon and Goodreads. We appreciate your positive and constructive feedback. Thank you.

Manufactured by Amazon.ca
Bolton, ON

35015488R00050